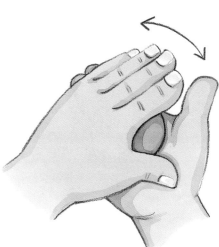

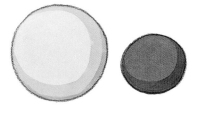

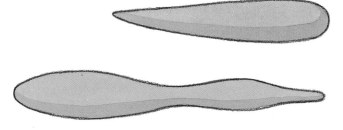

BALLS

A ball is made by placing the modeling clay in the palm of one hand and shaping it with the other one. Then you can mold it as you like: for example, by pinching it or by flattening it with your fingers or with a rolling pin to make a slab.

SAUSAGES

To make a sausage, place a piece of modeling clay on a table and, rolling the clay backward and forward, lengthen it with your fingers stretched out. To make a sausage with different widths, apply more pressure to some areas.

Basic techniques

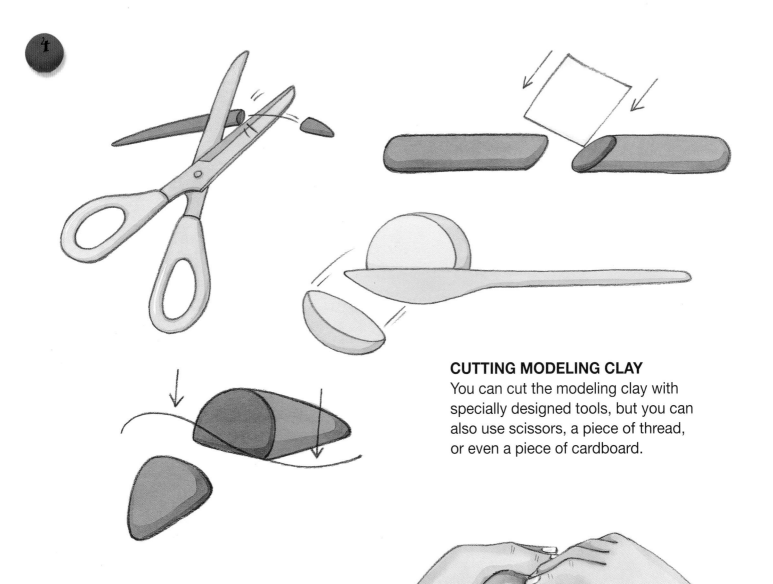

CUTTING MODELING CLAY
You can cut the modeling clay with specially designed tools, but you can also use scissors, a piece of thread, or even a piece of cardboard.

MIXING MODELING CLAY
To obtain different colors, you can mix two or more colors together with your hands. If you mix them a little, you will have a marbled effect. If you mix them completely, you will have a uniform color.

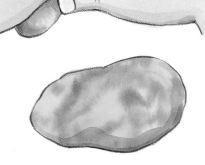

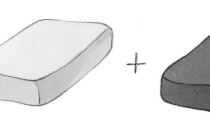

JOINTS

When you want to join two pieces together that might come unstuck (the head and body or the eyes and head), use a piece of toothpick to reinforce the joint. Where possible, secure the joint by smearing the modeling clay in that area, until the two pieces are joined together well (as on the animal's neck).

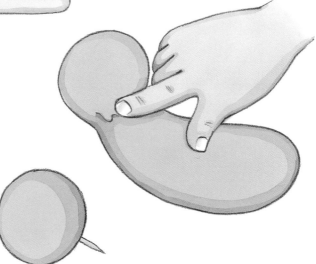

MOUTHS

You can make an open mouth with a piece of cardboard. If you want the mouth wide open, move the cardboard up and down before removing it. You can also make lips from little sausages.

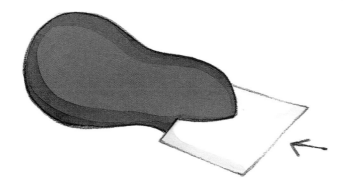

TEXTURES

You can press the clay with pieces of plastic tube, drinking straws, or lids to make different-sized circles. With a piece of mesh, you can create a texture of small squares to represent scales.

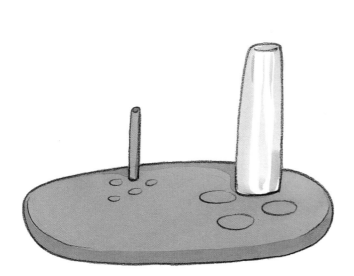

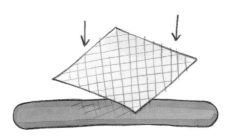

FINS AND TAILS

You can make fins, tails, antennae, and similar parts by cutting them out from such lighter materials as paper, cardboard, and scoubidous. You'll be surprised how well they stick into the modeling clay!

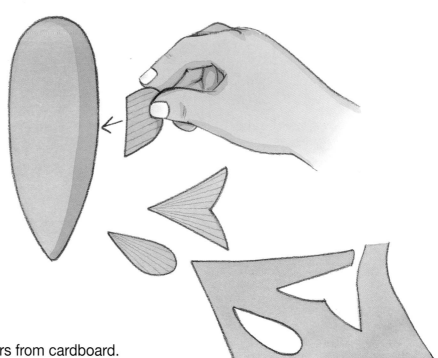

EARS

You can also make ears from cardboard. Cut out the shape and fold it a little at the tip before sticking it into the clay.

SPOTS AND STRIPES

For spots, spread a small amount of modeling clay over the animal. For stripes, make very thin sausages and press them onto the body. An easier way to make stripes is to paint over the modeling clay with enamel paint or nail polish. When you have finished, use a solvent to clean the paintbrushes.

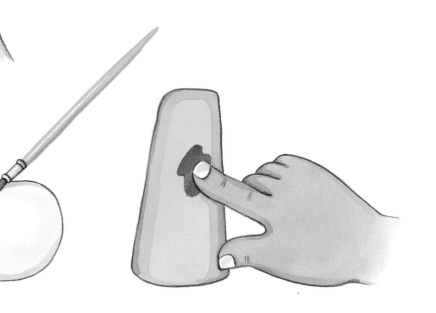

MANES AND TAILS

You can make a mane either by cutting a fringe in a strip of cardboard or by sticking pieces of wool onto a strip of sticky tape and folding it lengthwise. To make a tail, stick several pieces of wool onto one end of some sticky tape and roll it up.

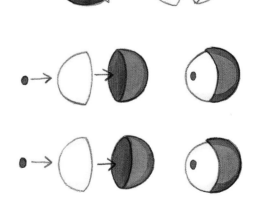

EYES

An easy way to make eyes is to form two different colored balls. Cut them in half and join the different-colored halves together. Flatten them a little and place small balls in the middle to make the pupils.

HAIRY COATS

To produce a hairy effect, cut short pieces of wool and roll the modeling clay in it until it is covered. Press very well.

Clown Fish

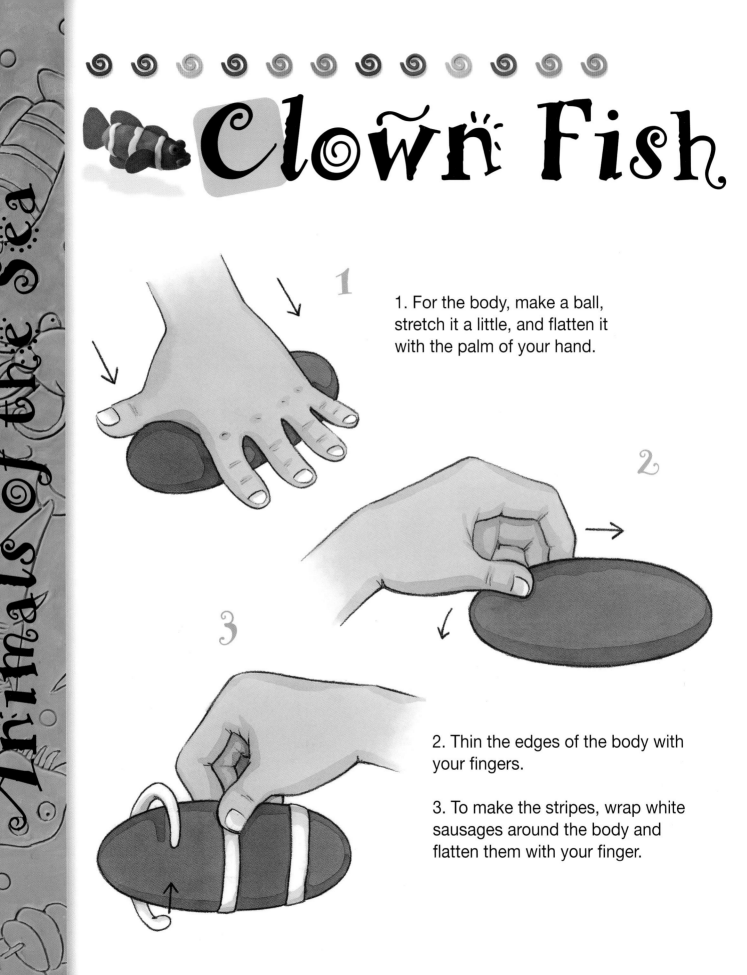

1. For the body, make a ball, stretch it a little, and flatten it with the palm of your hand.

2. Thin the edges of the body with your fingers.

3. To make the stripes, wrap white sausages around the body and flatten them with your finger.

4

4. For the eyes, stick two black balls onto larger ones and press the eyes firmly into the body.

5. Make two sausages for the lips.

5

6

6. Cut out the fins from a piece of cardboard and stick them into place.

Shapes and colors

In the sea, there are many fish with different markings: spots, patches, zigzag stripes...

Sea Urchin

1. Make a ball.

2. Use scissors to cut the tips off some toothpicks. Then cut them in half.

1

2

3. Throw the ball on a hard surface so that it stands upright. Then stick the toothpicks all over the ball.

3

Ouch!

Sea urchins live among the rocks. Try not to step on them: being pricked by their spines is very painful.

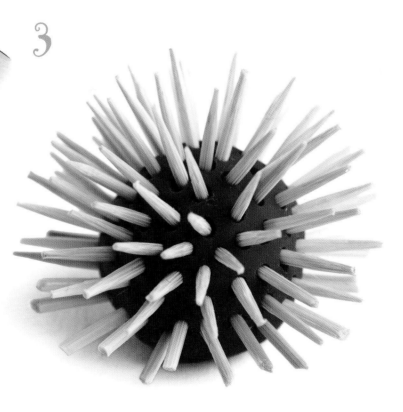

Starfish

1. Cut a sausage into five pieces and roll one end of each into a point.

2. Make two cuts at the wide end of each sausage to create an arrow shape. Join the cut ends together.

1

2

3

3. Press the joints with your finger to reinforce them. Use a scoubidou to make the pattern of little circles.

Crab

1. For the body, flatten half a ball with the palm of your hand.

2. Pinch one side with your fingers to give shape to the rear part.

3. For the eyes, make two balls the same color as the body with a small black ball in the middle of each. Make a mouth with a piece of cardboard.

4. Make two pointed sausages for the front legs. Using a piece of toothpick, join them firmly to the sides of the crab. Smooth the joints with your finger.

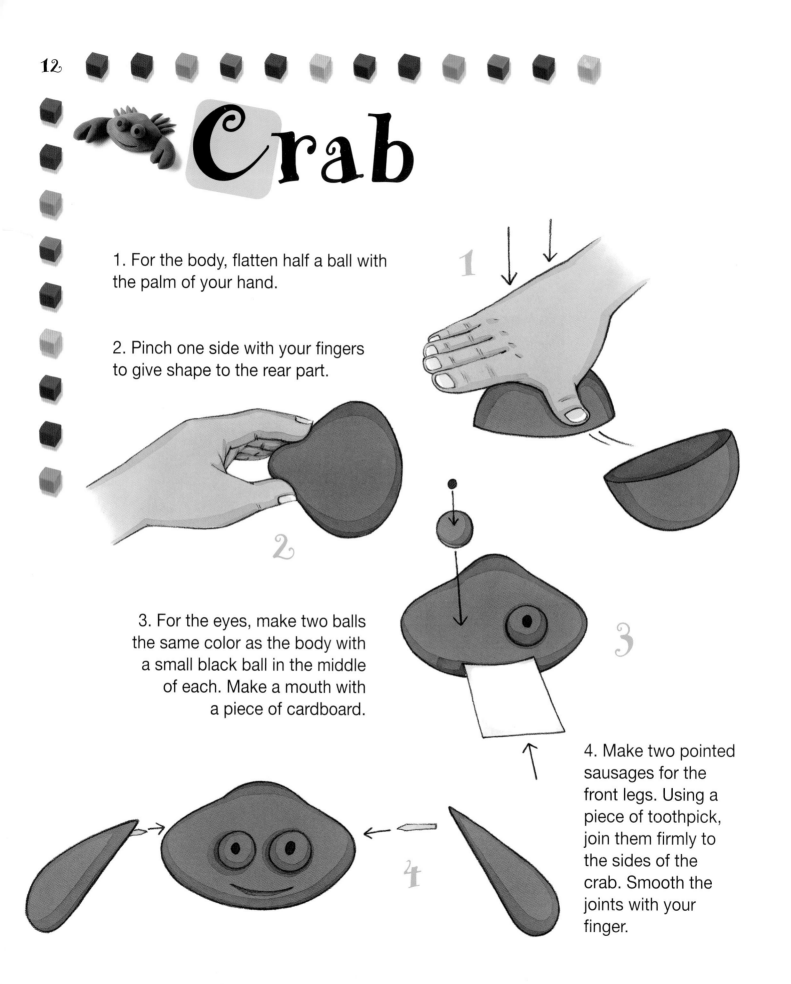

5

5. Use your fingers to flatten the front of these legs, called the pincers. Open them with a piece of cardboard.

6. Finally, make eight small sausages and place them behind the pincers, four on each side.

6

Walking backwards

It seems like we're putting his legs on his back, doesn't it? Crabs have their legs there because they only walk backwards or sideways.

Dolphin

1. For the body, make a large sausage with a point at one end. Then make two small sausages, one the same color and one a lighter color. Cut both lengthwise and discard half of each one.

2. Stick the two small pieces onto the round end of the sausage, placing the lighter one underneath. Blend the lighter piece along the belly.

3. Make two black balls for the eyes. Stick in the fins and tail, cut out from thick cardboard.

Jellyfish

1. Cut off the lower part of a ball and discard it. Pinch around the base.

2. Draw vertical stripes around the rim with a toothpick. Then mark some circles on the top with a pen lid.

3. Stick some thin strips of paper onto a sausage the same color as the ball. Roll the sausage into a ball and stick it underneath. Stick some long pieces of scoubidou around the paper.

Seahorse

1

1. For the body, make a sausage that is narrow in the middle and at both ends.

2. Form the head by bending the narrow midsection as shown and roll the tail inward.

3. Press the snout against a table to flatten it.

2

3

A peculiar fish

The seahorse, with its strange appearance and upright swimming position, is one of the strangest fish found in the marine world.

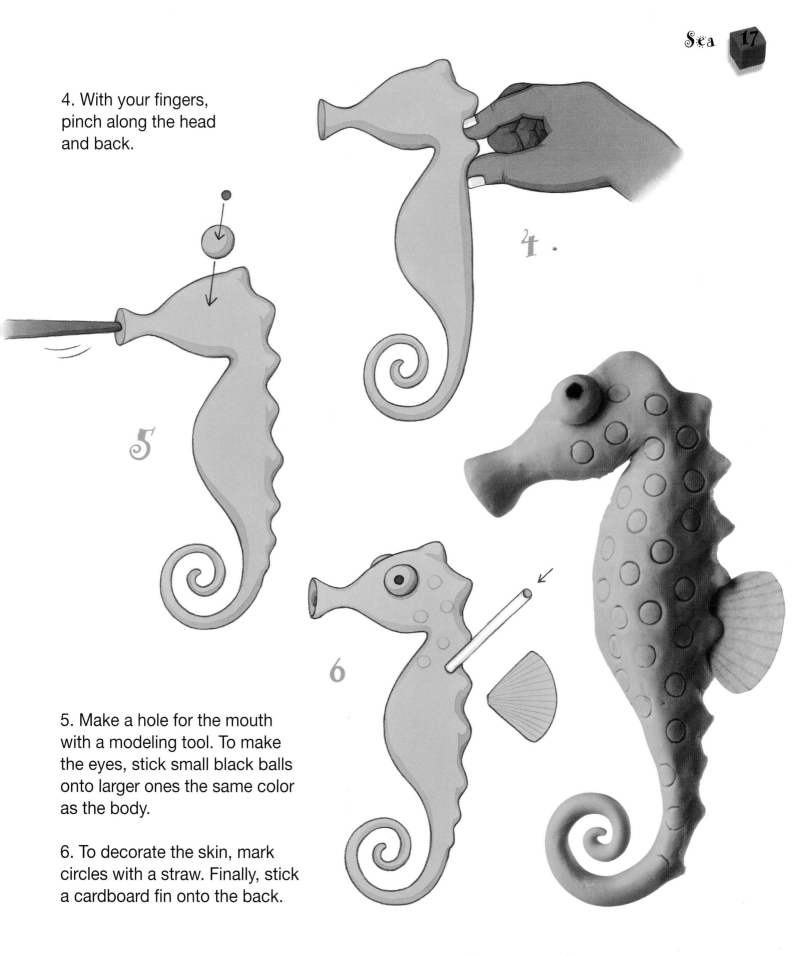

4. With your fingers, pinch along the head and back.

5. Make a hole for the mouth with a modeling tool. To make the eyes, stick small black balls onto larger ones the same color as the body.

6. To decorate the skin, mark circles with a straw. Finally, stick a cardboard fin onto the back.

Turtle

1. For the shell, make a ball of mixed colors and flatten it with the palm of your hand.

2. Make six different shapes: a thick round one for the head, four smaller ones for the legs, and a short pointed one for the tail.

3. Turn the shell over and stick these body parts onto the flat surface, which will be the underside of the turtle. Smooth the joints with your finger.

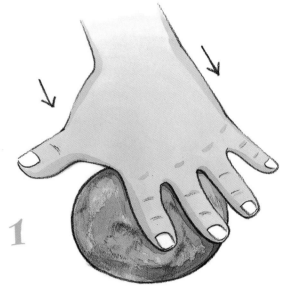

4. Turn the shell over and adjust the limbs. Lift the head and tail. To make a nose, pinch the head.

5. For the eyes, stick two small black balls onto two larger colored balls. Use a piece of cardboard to make the mouth.

6. Mark the toes on the feet with a skewer and decorate the shell with a pen lid.

Seagull

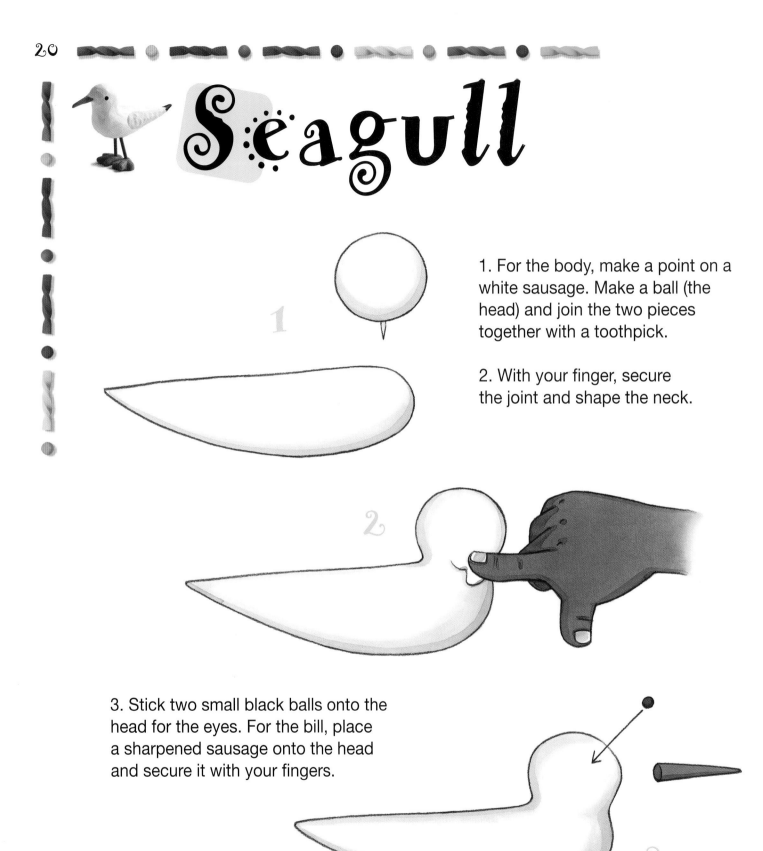

1. For the body, make a point on a white sausage. Make a ball (the head) and join the two pieces together with a toothpick.

2. With your finger, secure the joint and shape the neck.

3. Stick two small black balls onto the head for the eyes. For the bill, place a sharpened sausage onto the head and secure it with your fingers.

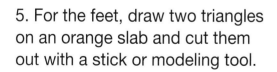

4. Stick a piece of black modeling clay on the tip of the tail. To make the wings, flatten a sausage of gray clay. Create the feather texture with your fingers.

5. For the feet, draw two triangles on an orange slab and cut them out with a stick or modeling tool.

6. Paint two pieces of skewer orange and stick them into the feet. Attach the skewer end to the seagull so that the animal stands up.

Octopus

1. Make an oval shape for the body and eight long sausages pointed at one end for the tentacles.

1

2. Join the sausages to one side of the ball with pieces of toothpick. Secure them with your fingers.

2

3

3. Give shape to the tentacles by coiling them in different directions. Try to make the tentacles look alive.

4

4. For the eyes, place two balls the same color as the octopus onto the head and add two tiny black balls for the pupils.

5. Make the mouth with a piece of cardboard.

5

6

6. Mark the suckers with a piece of plastic tube.

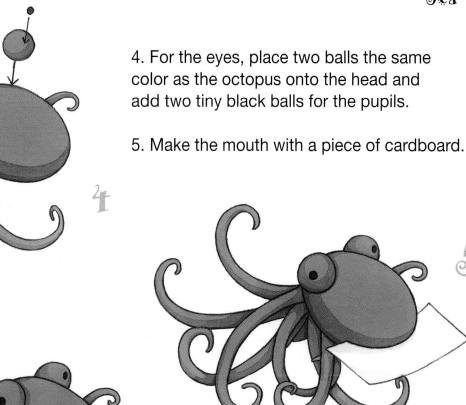

There's more...

If you like making tentacles, you can try making other animals that have them, such as squid.

Whale

1. For the body, make a sausage pointed at one end. Stick two small sausages to the largest end, one gray sausage and a white one.

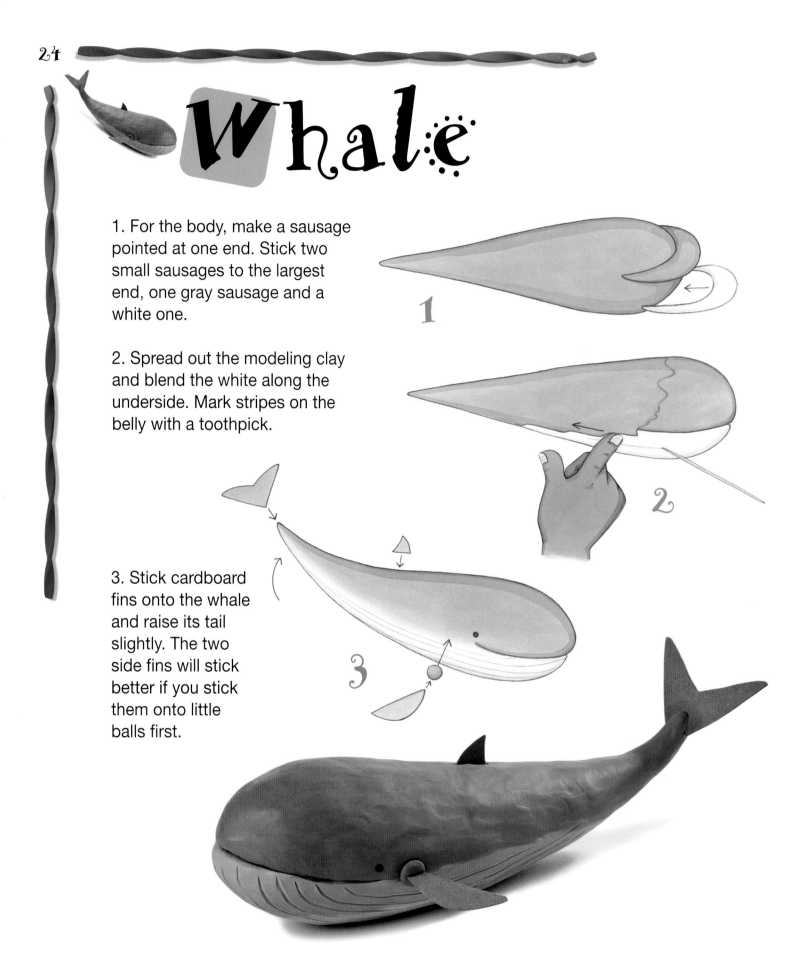

2. Spread out the modeling clay and blend the white along the underside. Mark stripes on the belly with a toothpick.

3. Stick cardboard fins onto the whale and raise its tail slightly. The two side fins will stick better if you stick them onto little balls first.

Angelfish

1. For the body, flatten a ball with the palm of your hand. Mold two rounded tips with your fingers.

2. Make the mouth with a piece of cardboard. For the eyes, stick two black balls onto two colored ones. Finish decorating the fish by pressing thin sausages onto its body with your fingers.

3. Cut out the fins and tail from greaseproof paper and stick them into place.

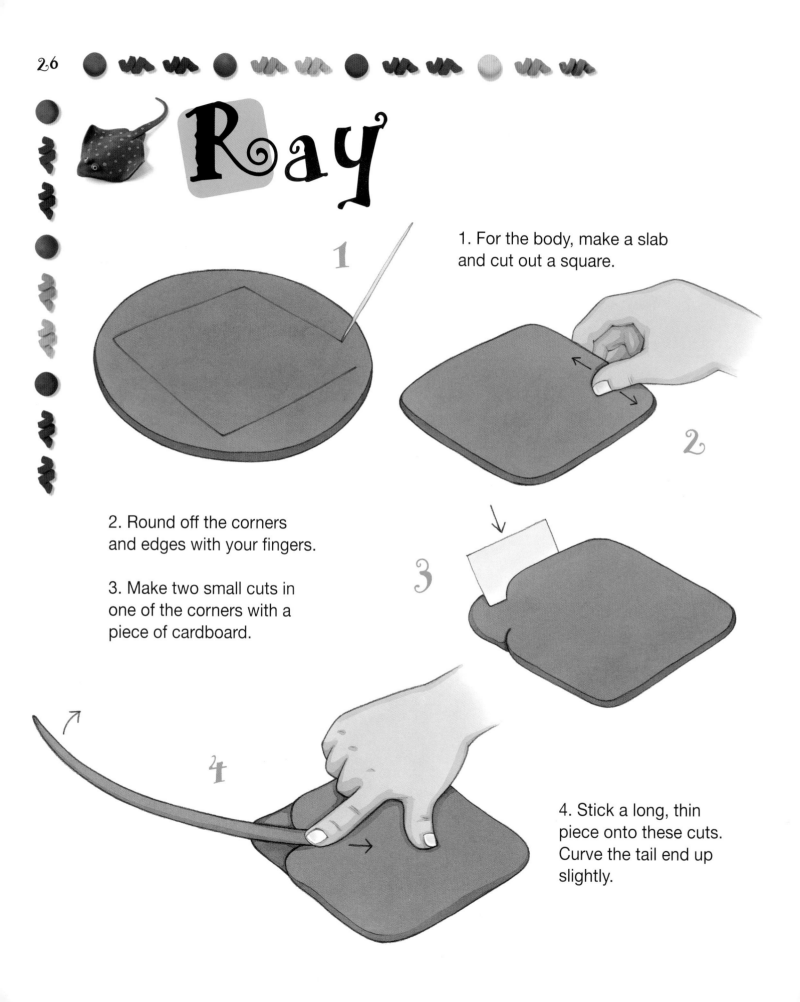

Ray

1. For the body, make a slab and cut out a square.

2. Round off the corners and edges with your fingers.

3. Make two small cuts in one of the corners with a piece of cardboard.

4. Stick a long, thin piece onto these cuts. Curve the tail end up slightly.

5. To make the eyes, stick three balls one over the other: A large one the same color as the ray, a medium-sized one in another color, and a final small black one. To make the spots, flatten small colored balls all over the body.

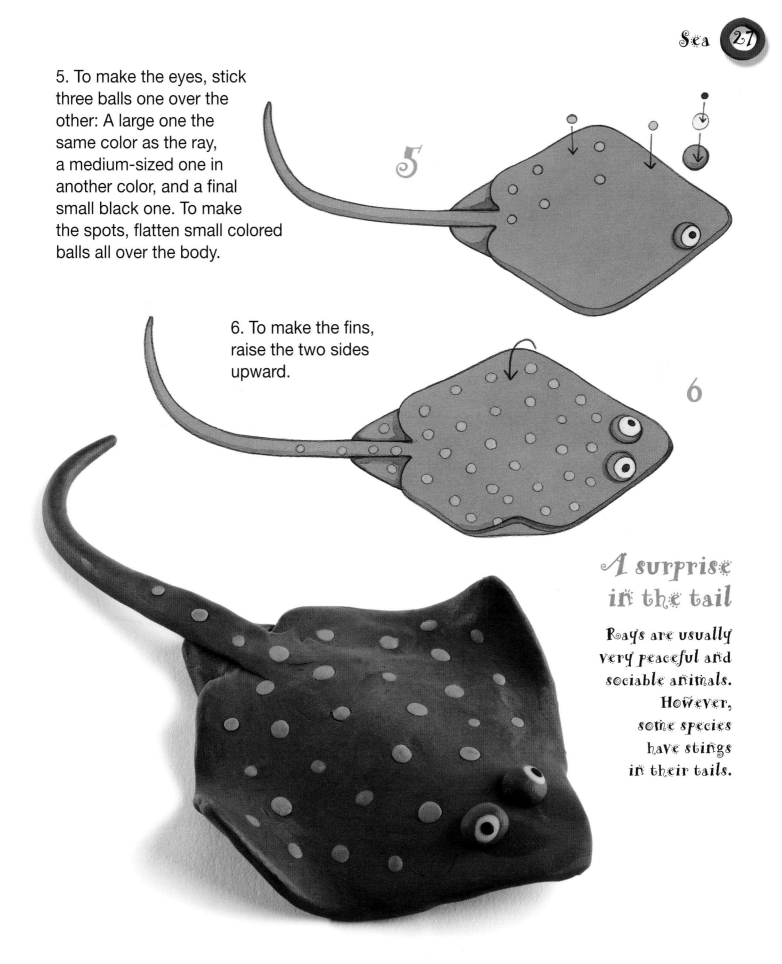

5

6. To make the fins, raise the two sides upward.

6

A surprise in the tail

Rays are usually very peaceful and sociable animals. However, some species have stings in their tails.

Shark

1

1. Make a sausage with a pointed narrow end and a pointed wider end.

2. Flatten a white sausage on the lower part to mark the belly. Smooth it out and blend it with the body.

2

3

3. Make the mouth and open it wide with a piece of cardboard.

4. Cut out teeth from a piece of white cardboard and stick them into the mouth opening.

4

5

5. To make the eyes, stick two yellow balls onto the head and flatten two tiny black sausages onto them for the pupils. Make two holes with a toothpick for the nostrils. Mark five lines on each side of the shark with a piece of cardboard.

6

Other species

By changing the shape of the head, you can make a ferocious hammerhead. Why not give it a try?

6. Cut out the tail and fins from a piece of cardboard. Stick them in place.

Flamingo

1. For the body, mold a ball into an almond shape. Make a sausage rounded at one end for the neck and head and bend it.

2. Join the neck to the body with a toothpick and secure the joint. Make the bill pieces and wings and secure them in place.

3. For the eyes, stick little black balls onto larger balls. Paint two pieces of skewer for the legs. Model the feet from two ball halves and stick them onto the skewers. Give texture to the wings with your fingers.

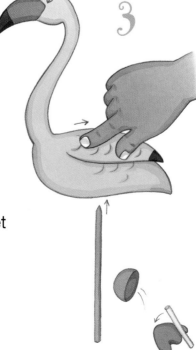

Chameleon

1. With a toothpick, join together a triangular shape for the head and a long pointed sausage for the body and tail. Press the pieces together firmly. Narrow the back with your fingers to form a crest. Pinch the upper part of the head. Curl the tail.

2. Make the mouth. For the bulging eyes, stick two small black balls onto larger balls. Make the legs from sausages and model the feet with a tool.

3. Make the crest along the spine with a tool. Use a piece of plastic tube to give texture to the whole body.

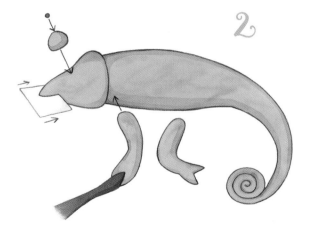

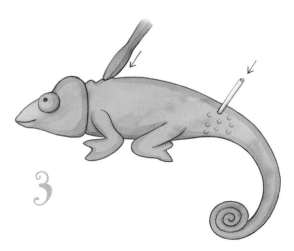

Hippopotamus

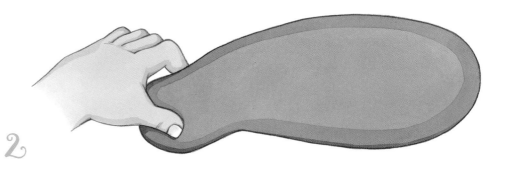

1. Mold the body and head shape from a very thick sausage. Bend the head downward slightly.

1

2

2. Pinch the upper center part of the head a little with your fingers.

3. To make skin folds, press two thin sausages onto the underside of the neck and blend them on both sides.

4. Stick two small black balls onto two larger ones to make the eyes. Flatten two more balls for the ears.

3

4

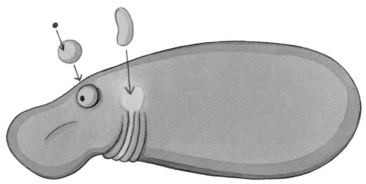

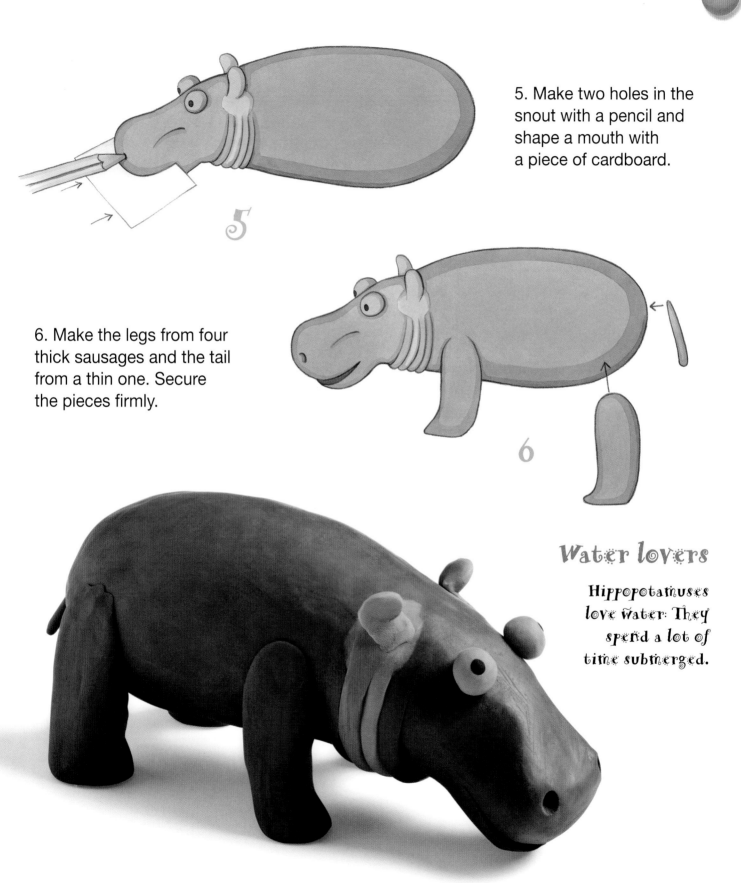

5. Make two holes in the snout with a pencil and shape a mouth with a piece of cardboard.

6. Make the legs from four thick sausages and the tail from a thin one. Secure the pieces firmly.

Water lovers

Hippopotamuses love water. They spend a lot of time submerged.

Lion

1. Make a small cone (the nose), a ball (the head), and a short sausage-shape (the body). Stick the nose onto the head and the head onto the body with a piece of skewer.

2. Secure the neck using your finger. Make three white balls for the cheeks and chin. Stick them underneath the nose.

3. Stick a flattened black ball on the base of the nose. Stick two balls onto the head for the ears.

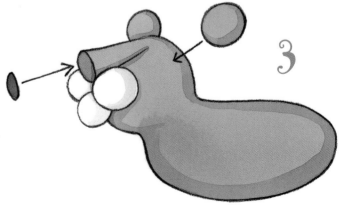

4. Use four sausage-shapes for the legs. Stick two on each side of the body. Secure them well and bend the ends to make the paws.

5. To make the eyes, stick a black ball onto each side of the nose. Roll a very thin tail and stick it on. Now you have a female lion.

6. For a male lion, make a mane by wrapping some wool around the neck.

Rhinoceros

1. Begin with two pieces: one for the head and another larger, rounder one for the body. Join them together with a toothpick and reinforce the joint.

2. Stick four sausages on the body for the legs. Model the feet a little so that the animal will be more stable.

3. Place a sausage on the upper part of the front legs and spread it upward. The tail is a thin sausage. Mark little hairs on it with a toothpick.

4. Stick two pointed sausages on the nose for the horns. For the eyes, stick two black balls on larger ones.

5. Mark the eyelids with a tube or lid and make the mouth with a piece of cardboard.

6. Mark the nostrils with the tip of a pencil. To finish, stick cardboard ears onto little gray balls.

An animal with a lot of character

The rhinoceros is very large and bad tempered. Luckily, it is also very shortsighted...

Snake

1

2

3

1. Roll out a long, thin sausage. Make a point at one end for the tail. Round off the other end to make the head.

2. For the eyes, stick two little black balls on small sausages. Make the nostrils with a toothpick.

3. Make the mouth with a piece of cardboard. Press a piece of mesh over the body for the scales. Finish by bending it into an S-shape.

Colorful snakes

There are many different types of snakes, with very different colors and markings. Instead of the mesh pattern, you could make colored patches.

Parrot

1. Make a sausage and mold the head and the tail. Flatten a different-colored ball on each side of the head.

2. Stick on two black balls for the eyes. Make the bill with two different-sized sausages, curved and narrowed at the ends. Flatten and narrow two sausages for the wings. Mark the tail feathers with a toothpick.

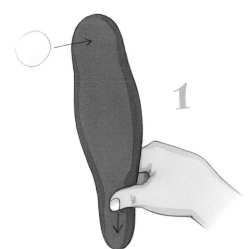

3. Use your fingers to create the wing texture. Make short legs and claws from small sausages and place your parrot on a clay branch.

Elephant

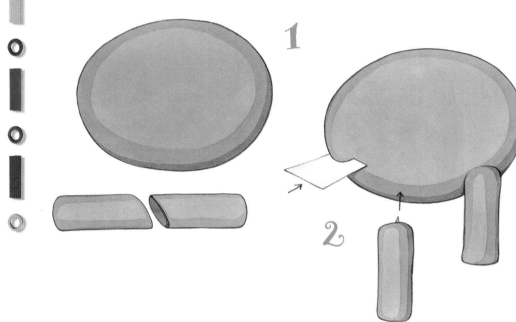

1. Make a large oval shape. Cut a long sausage into four equal pieces and cut one end of each piece diagonally so that the legs fit onto the body better.

2. Attach the legs with toothpicks. Make the mouth with a piece of cardboard.

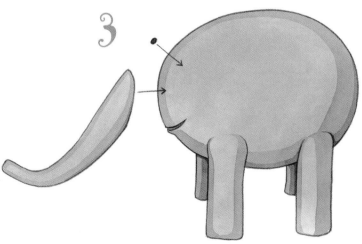

3. For the trunk, make a sausage that is thinner at one end. Stick it on above the mouth and secure it. Two little black balls will make the eyes.

4. Use a toothpick to mark some wrinkle lines on the trunk and make a hole in the end.

5. Mark the eyelids around the eyes with a tube or drinking straw. For the tusks, stick a pointed sausage on each side of the head.

6. A very thin sausage will do for the tail. To finish, cut out the large ears from cardboard and stick them on.

African or Indian?

African elephants have much larger ears than Indian ones. Where does your elephant come from?

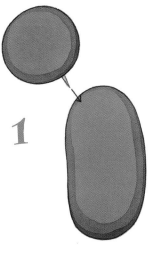

Chimpanzee

1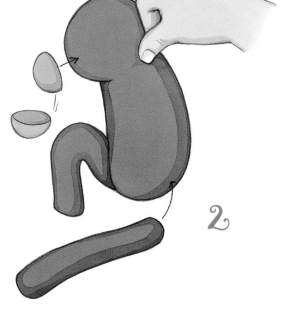

1. For the head and body, join a ball to a rounded sausage with a toothpick.

2. Secure the joint with your fingers. Stick two long sausages onto the base for the legs and half a pink ball onto the head for the mouth area.

2

3. Stick two slightly smaller balls above the mouth. Make two long sausages for the arms and stick them onto the body.

3

4. A small ball will do for the nose and two little black balls for the eyes. Make the mouth with a piece of cardboard and the ears from two half balls.

4

5

5. Use a toothpick to make two holes in the nose for the nostrils. Make each hand and foot from five very thin sausages joined together. Stick them in place.

6. Finish by marking lines all over the body with a toothpick for the hair.

6

Loyal companion

Tarzan's loyal companion Cheetah, a chimpanzee, accompanies him on all his adventures.

Tiger

1. Make a ball for the head and a rounded sausage for the body. Join them together with a toothpick.

2. Secure the joint with your fingers. Spread a lighter-colored sausage under the belly. Stick a smaller, pointed sausage on the head and flatten it for the nose.

3. Add a dark, flat piece of clay under the nose. Make the cheeks with two little balls and add a white one for the chin. Model two little balls on the head for the ears.

4. Make four sausages for the legs. Stick them onto the body and shape the feet.

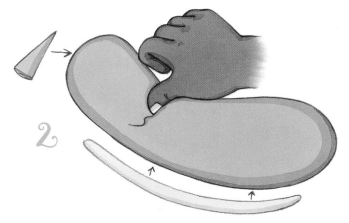

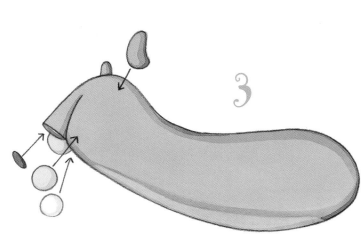

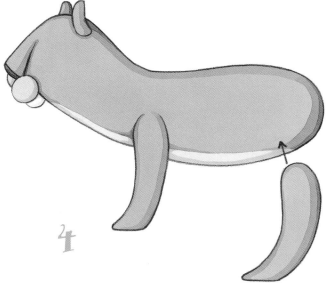

5. For the beard, cut a fringe on thin paper, make an opening in the neck, and stick it in. Stick two black balls over larger ones for the eyes. A thin sausage will do for the tail.

Changing the "design"

If you make spots instead of stripes, your tiger will become a leopard.

6. Add the stripes by pressing thin black sausages on the body or by painting them on.

Crocodile

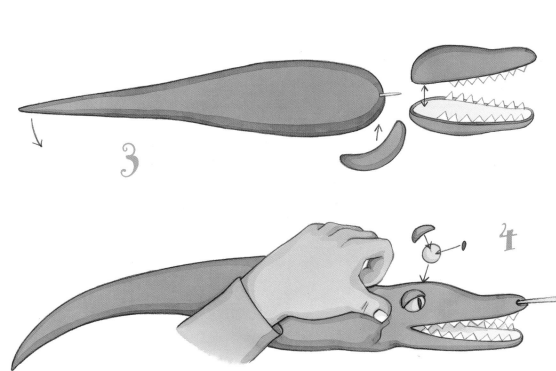

1. For the body, make a sausage pointed at one end. Make another smaller one for the head and cut it in half.

2. Cover the two flat sides of the head in pink modeling clay. Cut zigzags in two strips of cardboard for the teeth and stick them into the jaws.

3. Join the two parts of the head to the body with a toothpick and reinforce the joint with a sausage under the jaw.

4. Secure the joint well. For the eyes, stick two black balls onto larger yellow ones and make eyelids with little sausages. Make two holes in the nose.

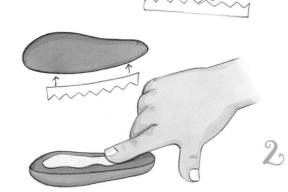

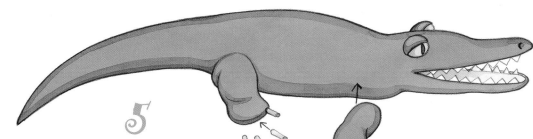

5. Mold four sausages for the legs. Use pieces of plastic tube for the claws.

6. Stick a thin sausage along the tail and mark the crest shape with a modeling tool. Finish by creating the skin texture with another tool.

Better not try it!

Holding a crocodile's mouth shut is easy despite its enormous size. Its jaw muscles are not very strong.

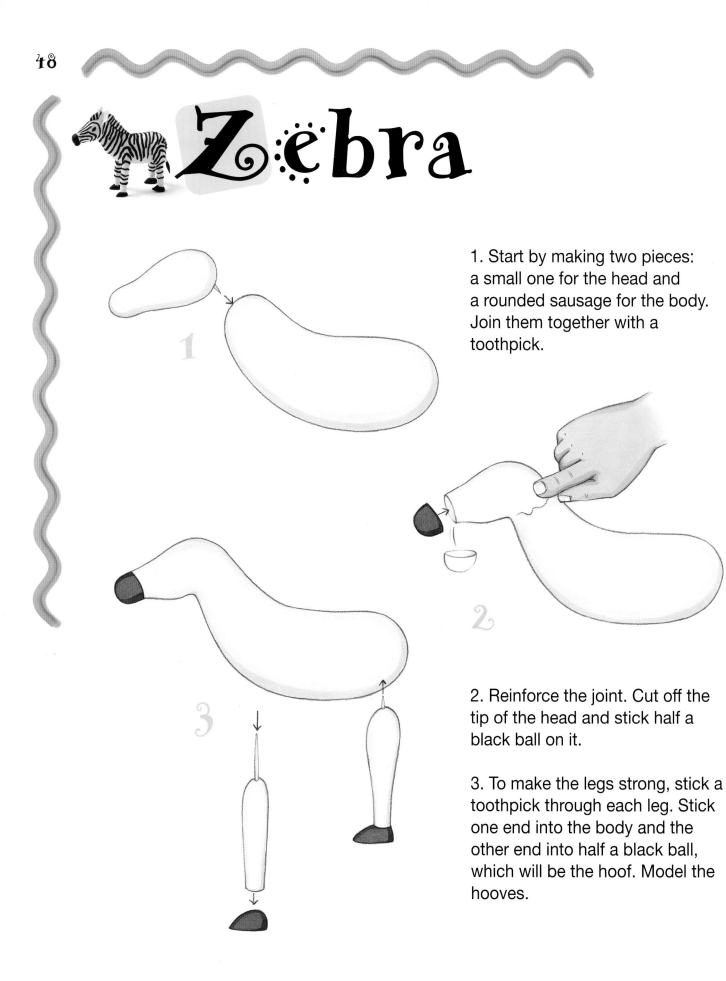

Zebra

1. Start by making two pieces: a small one for the head and a rounded sausage for the body. Join them together with a toothpick.

2. Reinforce the joint. Cut off the tip of the head and stick half a black ball on it.

3. To make the legs strong, stick a toothpick through each leg. Stick one end into the body and the other end into half a black ball, which will be the hoof. Model the hooves.

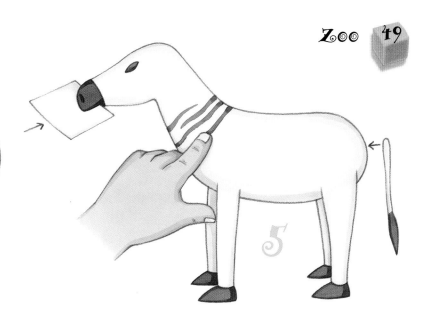

4. Make two holes in the nose with the tip of a pencil. Stick two little sausages onto the head for the eyes.

5. Make a white sausage with a black tip for the tail. Make the mouth with a piece of cardboard. For the stripes, flatten very thin black sausages over the body.

6. For the mane, paint some black stripes on a strip of white cardboard and cut a fringe in it. Stick it on the neck. Make the ears from cardboard and stick them in the head.

Giraffe

1. Mold three pieces: an elongated ball for the body, a sausage for the neck, and a smaller piece for the head.

1

2

2. Join them together with toothpicks and reinforce the joints with your fingers.

3

3. To make the legs, insert pieces of skewer into four sausages. Allow the tips to overhang and stick them into the body at one end and the hooves (half balls) at the other.

4. Use a tool to make nostrils and shape the mouth. Stick the tail on.

4

Reaching very high

The giraffe's long neck enables it to eat the highest leaves on the trees.

5. Stick a sausage on a ball for each eye and a little ball on a sausage for each horn. Make the ears from cardboard.

6. Spread patches over the body using small pieces of dark clay. Make a mane from a strip of folded, fringed paper and stick it into the neck.

Chick

1. Make a ball pointed at one end and another smaller ball. Join them together with a piece of toothpick and reinforce the joint with your fingers.

2. To make the wings, cut a flattened ball in half and stick a half on each side of the body. Stick the tip of a skewer painted orange into the head for the bill. Two small black balls will do for the eyes.

3. To make the legs and feet, mark the middle of a half ball. Stick two pieces of toothpick in it. Finally, stick the legs into the belly.

1

2

3

Goose

1. With a toothpick, join a sausage to a ball pointed at one end. Secure the joint and bend the neck slightly. Stick a flattened wing-shaped piece on each side.

2. Create the feather texture on the wings. Stick on a bill made from orange clay. Two black balls will do for the eyes.

3. Make two holes in the bill with a toothpick. To make each leg, insert a toothpick into a short sausage and stick one end into a clay triangle. Mark the toes with a toothpick.

Rabbit

1. Make two balls, one larger than the other. Flatten the base of the large ball slightly so that it stands up and stick the two balls together with a piece of skewer.

2. With your fingers, mold the nose on the upper ball (the head). To make the tail, stick a pointed ball onto the back end.

3. For the cheeks, stick two white balls underneath the nose. Stick another two small black balls onto the head for the eyes.

4. Cut out two cardboard ears and stick them into the upper part of the head.

5. With a skewer, make a hole for the mouth under the cheeks. For the back legs, stick two long sausage shapes under the body.

5

i'm hungry!

Why not shape an orange sausage into a carrot for your rabbit?

6. Stick another two sausages onto the body to make the front legs. Press firmly with your fingers. Make some whiskers by sticking some pieces of fishing line onto the cheeks.

6

Pig

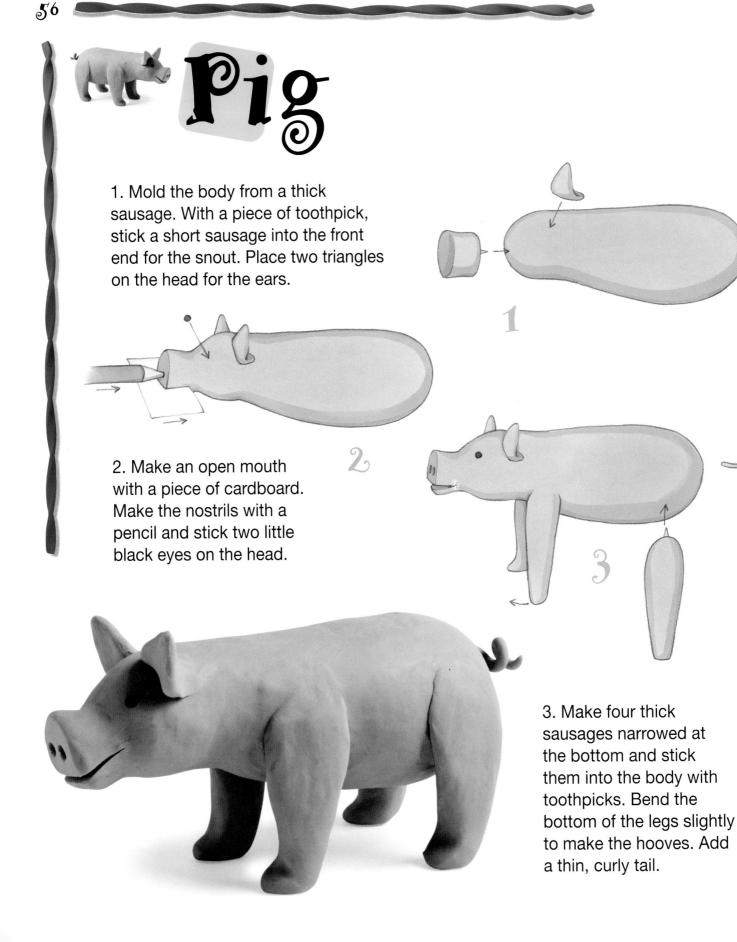

1. Mold the body from a thick sausage. With a piece of toothpick, stick a short sausage into the front end for the snout. Place two triangles on the head for the ears.

2. Make an open mouth with a piece of cardboard. Make the nostrils with a pencil and stick two little black eyes on the head.

3. Make four thick sausages narrowed at the bottom and stick them into the body with toothpicks. Bend the bottom of the legs slightly to make the hooves. Add a thin, curly tail.

Mouse

1. Make a ball pointed at one end. Stick on three small balls of the same size in a triangular pattern. The two lower balls should be the same color and the upper one a different color.

2. Stick white cardboard teeth under the balls. Two small balls will make the eyes. Stick little sausages under the body for the legs.

3. Bend the front legs slightly so that the body stands up. Stick some cardboard ears into the head. Make the tail from a piece of plastic tube.

1

2

3

Sheep

1. Make a head and an oval shape for the body. Join them together with a toothpick.

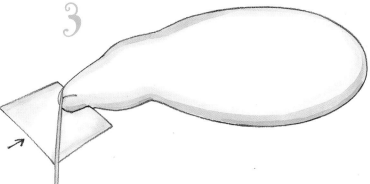

2. Secure and narrow the joint. Make two hollows for the eyes with your fingers.

3. Use a toothpick to mark a "Y" at the nose area. With a piece of cardboard, make an open mouth under the nose area.

4. Make holes for the nostrils. Stick small black balls onto larger white ones to make the eyes and place them in the hollows. Cut out two cardboard ears and stick them in the head.

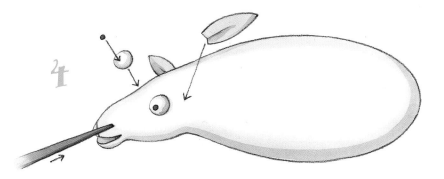

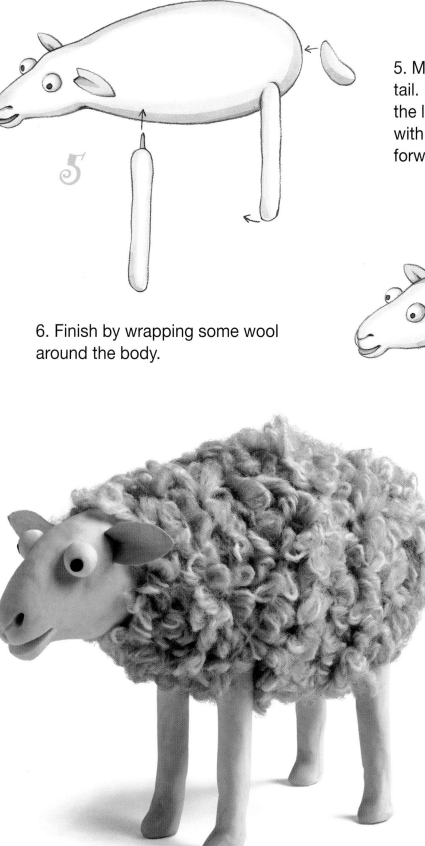

5. Model a small sausage for the tail. Make four thin sausages for the legs and stick them in the belly with toothpicks. Bend the feet forward slightly.

6. Finish by wrapping some wool around the body.

White or black?

Sheep can be different colors. Try wrapping your sheep in black, brown, or gray.

Dog

1. Begin by shaping three different-sized sausages: the head, the neck, and the body.

2. Secure and smooth the joints with your fingers. Flatten the nose.

3. Mark a vertical line in the nose area and below it make an open mouth. Secure a piece of clay on each side of the head for the ears.

4. To make the tongue, place a flat red piece in the mouth. Use a small black ball for the nose and two smaller balls for the eyes. If you want an eye patch, remember to put it in place before you stick the eye on.

Lots of breeds

You probably know different breeds of dogs. Now that you can make a dog, try to make a breed you know.

5

6

5. To make the legs, stick four sausages into the body with toothpicks. Bend the sausages slightly to make the feet.

6. Secure a small sausage for the tail. You can make patches by flattening different-colored pieces of clay on the body.

Cat

1. Join together a ball and a rounded sausage with a piece of toothpick.

2. Secure and smooth the joint. To make the nose, stick a pointed sausage onto the head and add a piece of pink modeling clay to the tip.

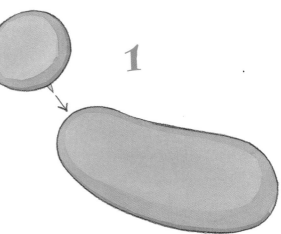

1

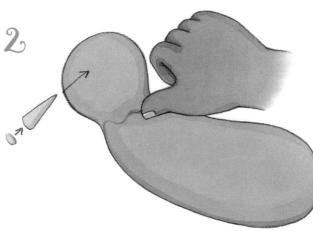

2

A cat has nine lives...

Cats can see very well in the dark. They are also very agile and quiet. They almost always land on their feet, and that's why they are said to have nine lives.

3

3. To make the face, stick two little balls on the sides of the nose and another smaller one under these two balls. Make the eyes by sticking tiny, elongated black sausages onto flat yellow balls.

4. Stick in two triangular clay ears. Mold the front legs and insert toothpicks into them. Secure the legs to the body and shape the feet.

5. To make the back legs, stick two sausages underneath two flattened balls. Secure the joints.

6. Stick some whiskers made from fishing line into the cheeks. Paint stripes on the cat.

Hen

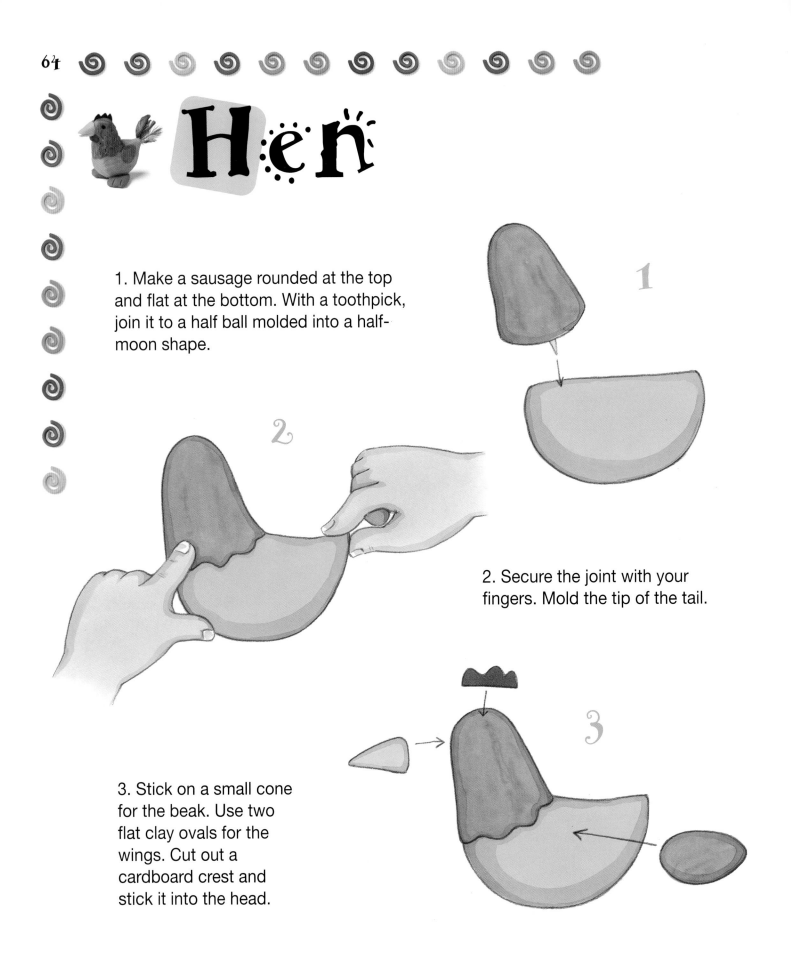

1. Make a sausage rounded at the top and flat at the bottom. With a toothpick, join it to a half ball molded into a half-moon shape.

2. Secure the joint with your fingers. Mold the tip of the tail.

3. Stick on a small cone for the beak. Use two flat clay ovals for the wings. Cut out a cardboard crest and stick it into the head.

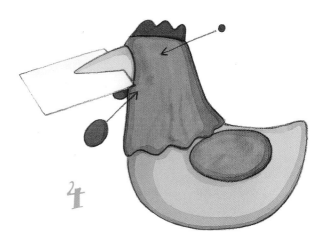

4. Open the beak with a piece of cardboard. Stick two red balls underneath the beak for the jowl. Use two small black balls for the eyes.

5. To make the legs, cut out two triangles from a sheet of modeling clay and stick them into the body with toothpicks. Stick some feathers in the tail.

6. To finish, use a toothpick to mark the toes on the feet and the feather texture.

Rooster

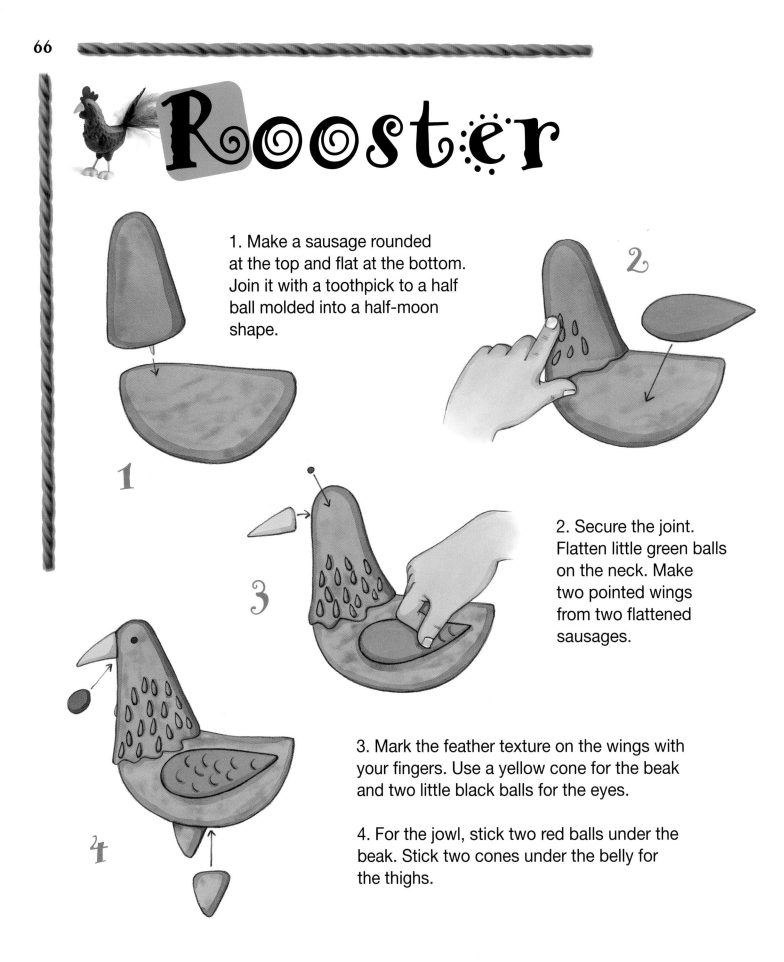

1. Make a sausage rounded at the top and flat at the bottom. Join it with a toothpick to a half ball molded into a half-moon shape.

2. Secure the joint. Flatten little green balls on the neck. Make two pointed wings from two flattened sausages.

3. Mark the feather texture on the wings with your fingers. Use a yellow cone for the beak and two little black balls for the eyes.

4. For the jowl, stick two red balls under the beak. Stick two cones under the belly for the thighs.

5

5. To make the legs, stick two pieces of skewer into clay triangles. Model the toes and then stick the legs into the thighs.

6

6. Cut out a large cardboard crest and stick it in the head. Stick some different-colored feathers on the tail.

Very jealous animals

It's best not to put two roosters in a henhouse. They are very jealous and territorial, and they'll spend the whole day fighting!

Donkey

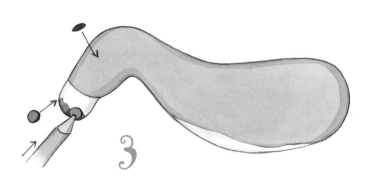

1. Use a toothpick to join together a small rounded sausage and a thicker longer one.

2. Secure and smooth the joint. Spread a white sausage over the belly. Cut off the tip of the nose and stick half a white ball in its place. Press a small piece of dark clay onto the white.

3. Stick two little dark balls on the nose and make a hole in each. Use two little black sausages for the eyes.

4. Make the mouth with a piece of cardboard. For the legs, insert skewers into four sausages and stick them in the belly. Secure the joints.

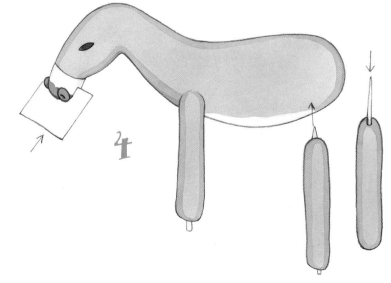

5. At the base of each leg, blend a white sausage upward. To make the hooves, stick a half ball onto the base of each leg.

They eat grass

Donkeys are herbivores, animals that eat plants.

6. To make the tail, stick on a sausage with a black tip. Stick some large cardboard ears into the head. To make the mane, cut a fringe on a strip of cardboard and stick it along the neck and back.

Horse

1. With pieces of toothpick, join three shaped sausages together: the head, the neck, and the body.

2. Secure and smooth the joints. With your fingers, define the shape of the belly at the front and back.

3. Make the mouth. Form the two nostril holes with a pencil.

4. Use two small black sausages for the eyes. Place a colored sausage above each eye for the eyelid. Stick two cardboard ears on the head.

5. Model four thin sausages for the legs and insert skewers in them. Stick triangles on the bottom of the legs for the hooves.

6. For the tail, stick pieces of wool together at one end of some sticky tape. Roll the tape into a point and stick it in the back end. To make the mane, stick small pieces of wool onto a long strip of sticky tape. Fold the tape lengthwise and stick it onto the neck.

They sleep standing up

It's very rare to see a horse lying down. They even sleep standing up.

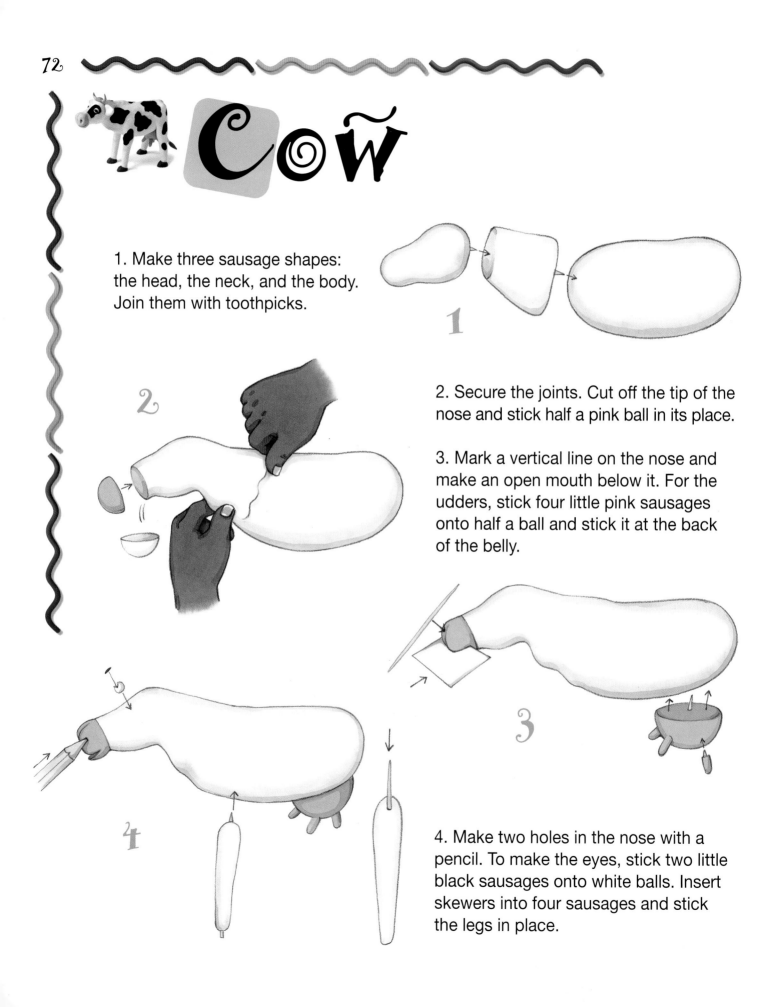

Cow

1. Make three sausage shapes: the head, the neck, and the body. Join them with toothpicks.

1

2

2. Secure the joints. Cut off the tip of the nose and stick half a pink ball in its place.

3. Mark a vertical line on the nose and make an open mouth below it. For the udders, stick four little pink sausages onto half a ball and stick it at the back of the belly.

3

4

4. Make two holes in the nose with a pencil. To make the eyes, stick two little black sausages onto white balls. Insert skewers into four sausages and stick the legs in place.

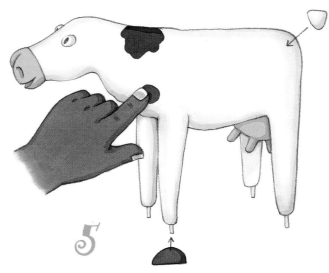

5. For the hooves, stick a half ball on the bottom of each leg. Stick two small cones above the back legs. Make the patches by flattening black pieces of clay.

6. Use a sausage with a dark tip for the tail. To make the horns, stick a little sausage on the head and add a curved pointed cone at each end. Mold two small triangles for the ears.

Large producers

Most of the milk drunk by humans comes from cows.

Caterpillar

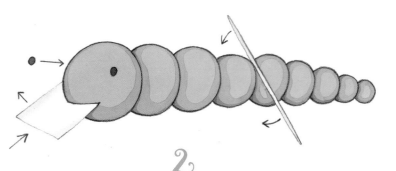

1. Make nine or ten balls, each one smaller than the last. Place toothpicks through them to join them all together.

2. Define the joints with a toothpick or modeling tool. Make an open mouth with a piece of cardboard and stick on two small black balls for the eyes.

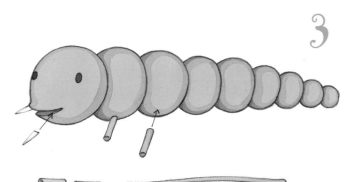

3. Cut out two small triangles from white cardboard and stick them inside the mouth. To make the legs, stick in small pieces of plastic tube.

Butterfly

1. Model a sausage slightly thicker at one end and join it to a ball. Mark lines on the thin part of the sausage and curve it downward.

2. Stick an eye on each side of the head. Make the antennae from two plastic tubes with little balls on the ends. Make the mouth hole with a pencil.

3. Cut out wings from cardboard and decorate them. Stick them into the thorax. A piece of plastic tube on the head will do for the sucking snout. Make the legs from toothpicks.

Spider

1. Make a ball and roll it firmly in some pieces of wool so that they stick to it.

2. Make a smaller ball and join it to the large one with a piece of skewer.

3. Make two small balls for the eyes: one white and the other the same color as the body. Cut them in half and join the different-colored halves together. Add a tiny black ball to each eye for the pupils.

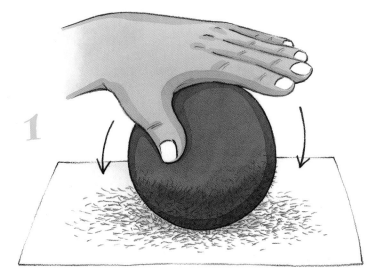

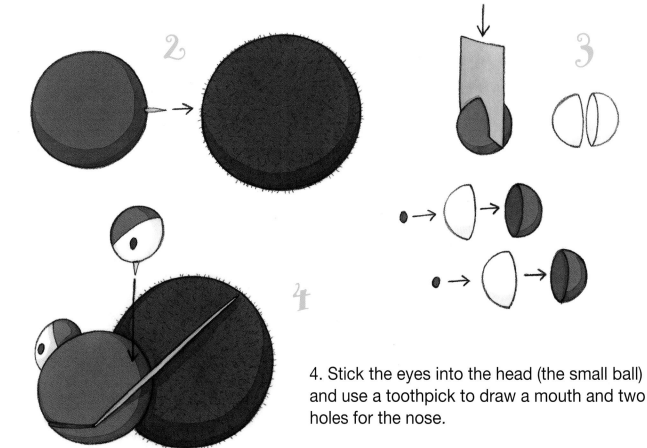

4. Stick the eyes into the head (the small ball) and use a toothpick to draw a mouth and two holes for the nose.

5. Cut out two white cardboard triangles and stick them into the mouth.

6. To make the legs, bend eight pipe cleaners and stick four into each side of the body.

Eight legs

Remember that spiders have eight legs, which you can make as long as you like.

Ladybug

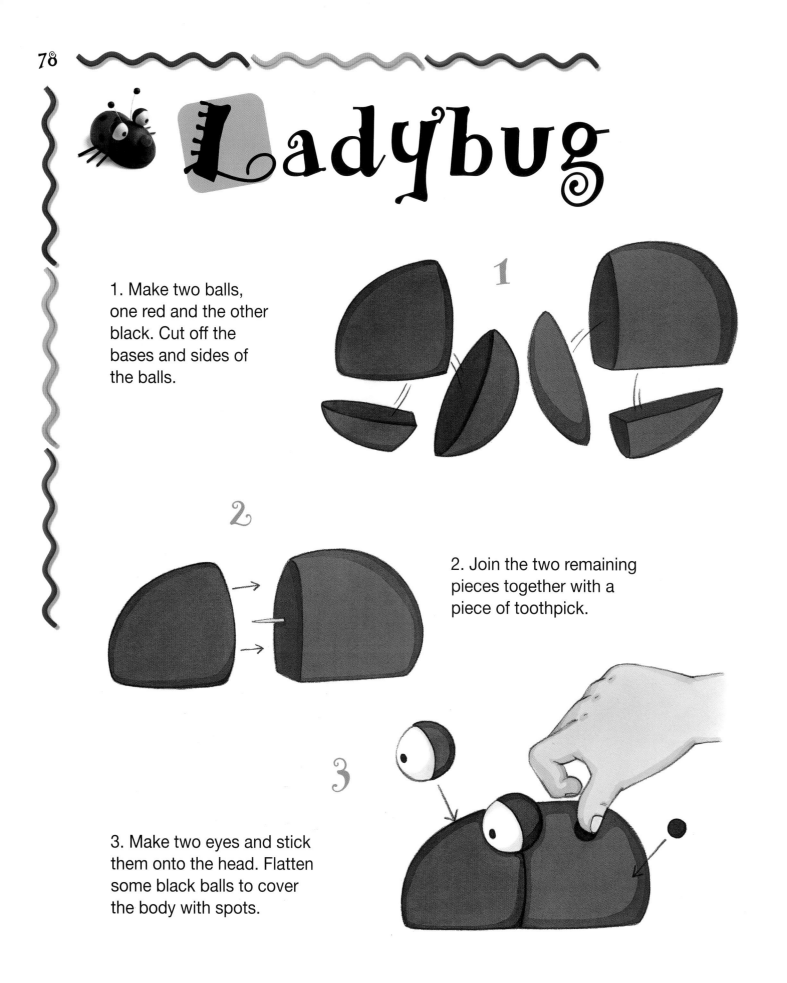

1. Make two balls, one red and the other black. Cut off the bases and sides of the balls.

2. Join the two remaining pieces together with a piece of toothpick.

3. Make two eyes and stick them onto the head. Flatten some black balls to cover the body with spots.

4

4. Use a toothpick to mark a line along the middle of the back. Make a slightly open mouth with a piece of cardboard.

5. Stick on a little ball for the nose. Make the antennae from two pieces of fishing line with little balls at the ends.

5

6

6. Cut out six pieces of plastic tube for the legs and stick three into each side. If you are feeling creative, you can make some eyelashes from small strips of cardboard.

Beetle

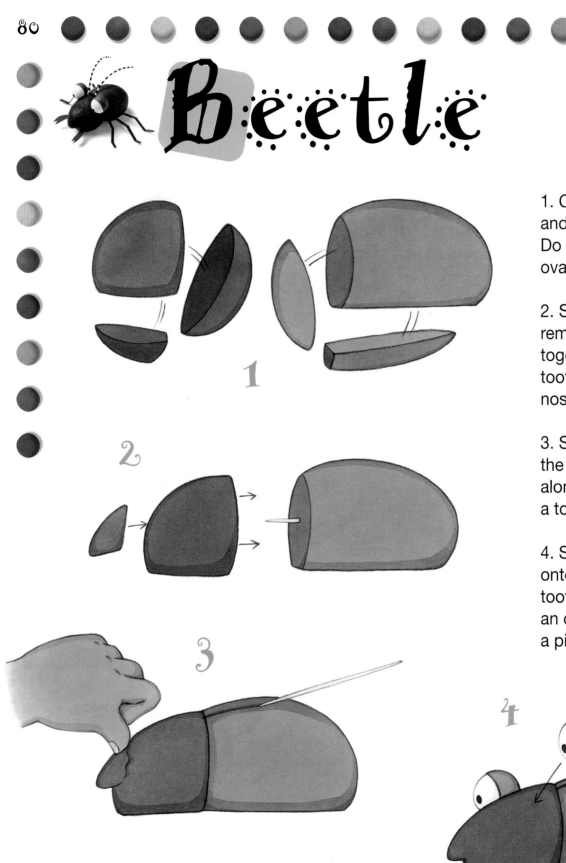

1

2

3

4

1. Cut off the base and side of a ball. Do the same to an oval.

2. Stick the two remaining pieces together with a toothpick. Make the nose from a triangle.

3. Secure and sharpen the nose. Mark a line along the back with a toothpick.

4. Stick the eyes onto the head with a toothpick and make an open mouth with a piece of cardboard.

5

5. Cut some pincers out of cardboard and stick them onto the head. For the antennae, draw stripes on two pieces of plastic tube with a felt-tipped pen and stick them into the head.

6. Use cardboard strips to make the legs. Fold them as shown and stick three into each side of the body.

6

Hidden Wings

Not everyone knows that beetles and ladybugs can fly. Their wings are hidden under their shell and come out only when needed.

Snail

1. Mold two different-colored sausages, each with a thinner end. Lift up the thickest end of the sausage that will be the body. For the shell, cut off the thick end of the other sausage and roll it up.

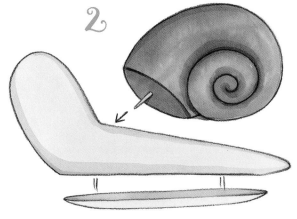

2. Cut the base off the body so that it stands up better. Stick on the shell with a toothpick.

3. Stick a small sausage across the base of the shell. Make a nose and place it on the head.

4

5

4. Secure the nose joint. Use a modeling tool to make the mouth opening.

5. Cut off two pieces of plastic tube and stick an eye onto each end. Then stick the other end into the head.

6

6. To finish, stick two smaller pieces of plastic tube under the nose.

Ant

1. Model two pointed balls and a small round one. Join them together, placing the small ball in the middle.

1

2. Make a mouth with a piece of cardboard. Stick the eyes onto the head and secure them with pieces of toothpick. Use a toothpick to mark stripes on the abdomen.

2

3

3. Make two antennae by sticking little balls of clay onto the ends of two pieces of fishing line. Cut out pieces of plastic tube to make the legs.

Mosquito

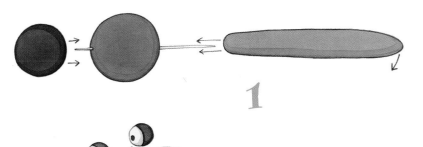

1

1. Model a sausage and two different-sized balls. Join the three pieces together, placing the large ball in the middle.

2. Stick two eyes onto the head with pieces of toothpick. Stick on a piece of plastic tube for the sucking snout and press half a white ball under it for the mouth.

2

3

3. Mark the mouthparts with a toothpick. Make the legs from pieces of plastic tube. Cut out two wings from parchment paper and stick them into the back.

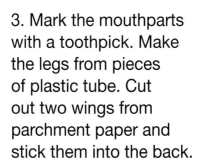

Wasp

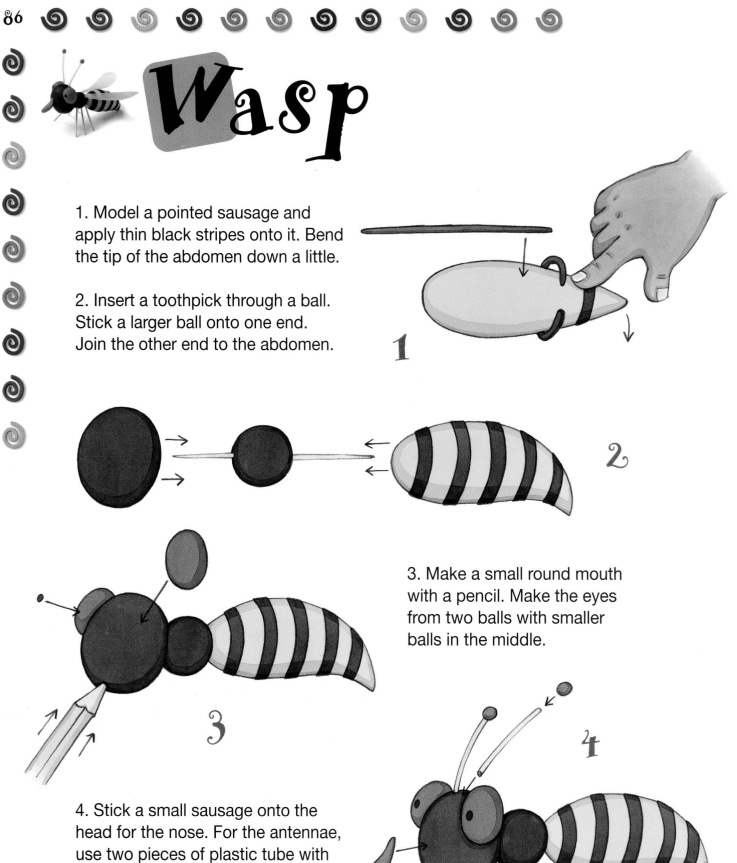

1. Model a pointed sausage and apply thin black stripes onto it. Bend the tip of the abdomen down a little.

2. Insert a toothpick through a ball. Stick a larger ball onto one end. Join the other end to the abdomen.

3. Make a small round mouth with a pencil. Make the eyes from two balls with smaller balls in the middle.

4. Stick a small sausage onto the head for the nose. For the antennae, use two pieces of plastic tube with balls on the ends.

5. Stick three pieces of toothpick onto each side of the thorax for the legs.

6. Cut out two wings from parchment paper. Color them with felt-tipped pens and stick them into the upper part of the thorax.

5

6

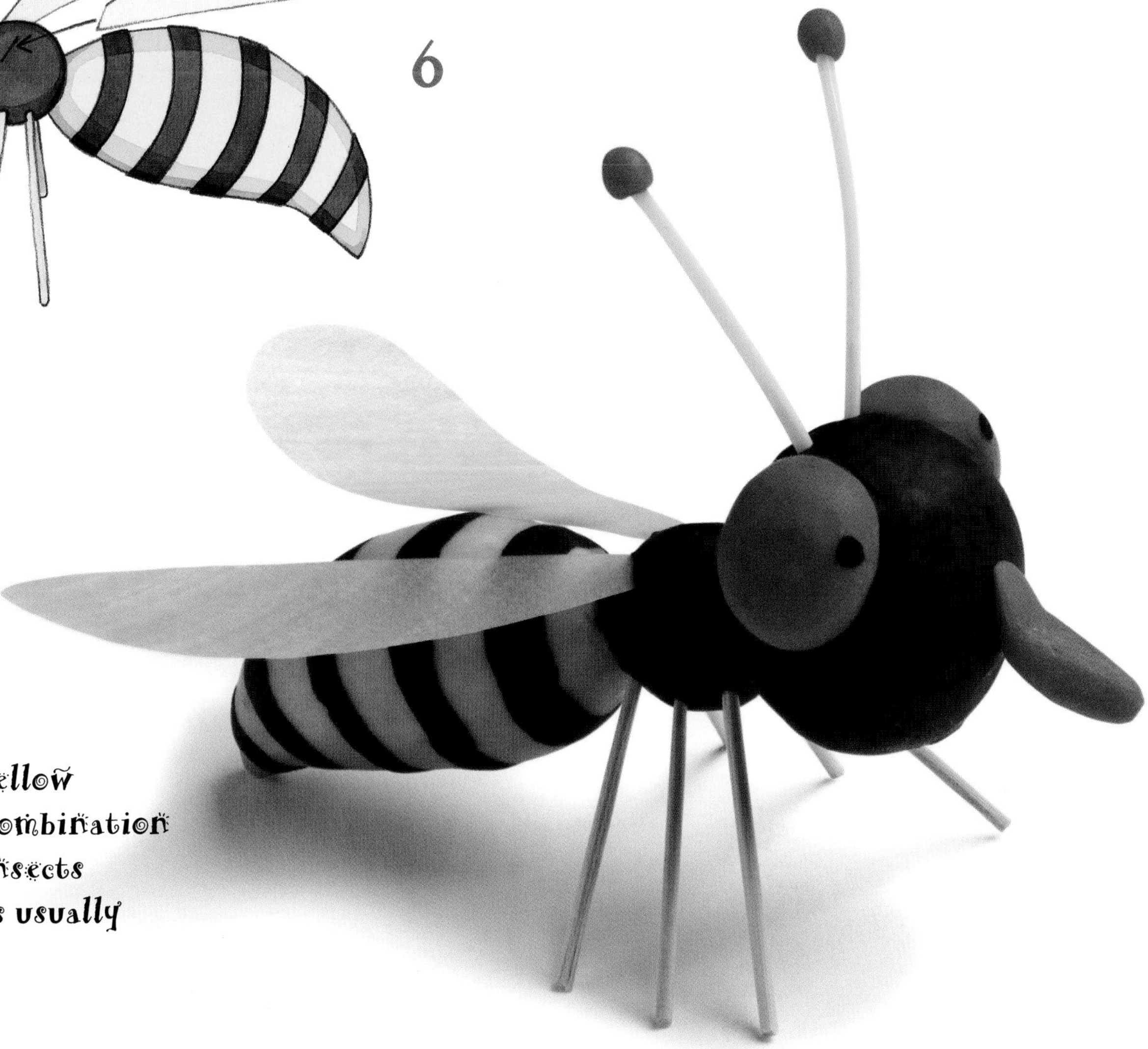

Danger!

In nature, the yellow and black color combination means danger. Insects with these colors usually sting.

Fly

1. Make a ball and a sausage pointed at one end and cover them in wool. Cut off the rounded end of the sausage.

2. Join the two pieces together with a toothpick and add a larger ball.

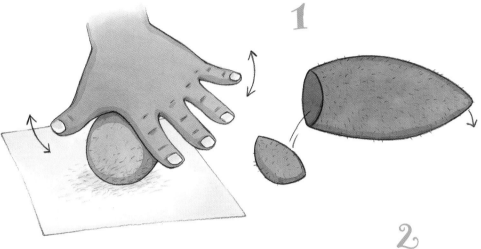

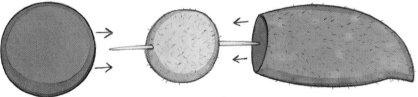

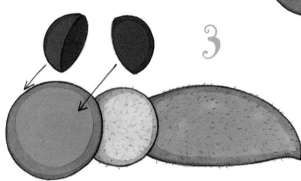

3. Cut a small ball in half and stick a piece onto each side of the head for the eyes.

4. Stick three small black balls onto each eye and flatten them. Make a sucking snout with a wide tip and stick it into the lower part of the head. Secure the joint.

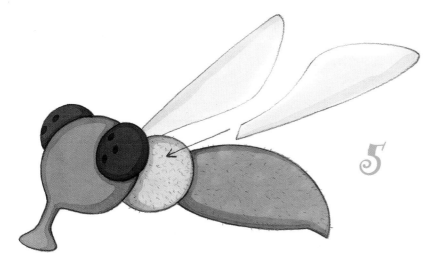

5

They eat everything

Flies never stop looking for food. With their snout, they taste the surface wherever they land. How bothersome they are!

5. Cut two wings out of parchment paper and stick them into the middle ball.

6

6. To make the legs, cut six pieces of plastic tube and stick three into each side of the thorax.

Frog

1. Make a thick rounded sausage and blend a smaller, lighter-colored one onto it. Bend it 90°, as shown.

2. For the back legs, stick a ball onto each side of the base.

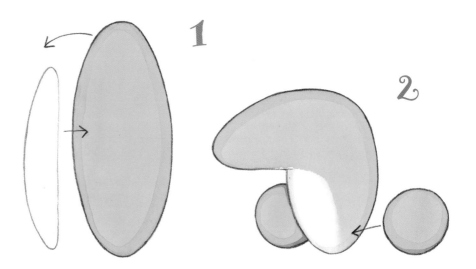

3. With a toothpick, mark the thigh folds. Cut out two rectangles from a clay slab for the feet. Stick them under the legs with pieces of toothpick.

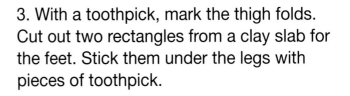

4. Make the front legs from two bottle-shaped sausages. Stick a flattened ball on the end of each one. Stick the legs into the body with pieces of toothpick.

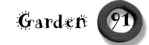

5. Stick on the eyes and make the mouth with a piece of cardboard. Use a toothpick to make the nostril holes.

6. To finish, make the fingers and toes. Stick four small pieces of plastic tube into each of the front legs. Do the same with the back legs and then stick small clay balls onto the ends.

And now ... a toad

If you use dark-green modeling clay and flatten little balls all over the body, it will look like a toad!

Lizard

1

1. Make two pieces:
an oval for the head and
a long sausage pointed
at one end for the body.
Join them together with
a toothpick.

2. Secure the joint.
Make the mouth with
a piece of cardboard.

2

3. Stick two eyes onto the head and make
two nostril holes with a toothpick.

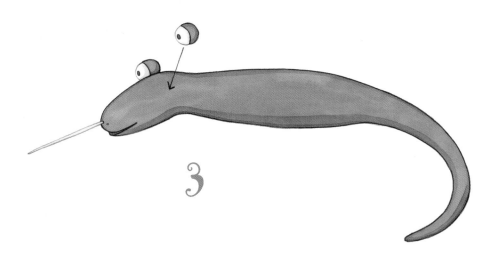

3

An escape artist

If you grab a lizard, you might end up with only its tail. A lizard's tail breaks off but grows back again.

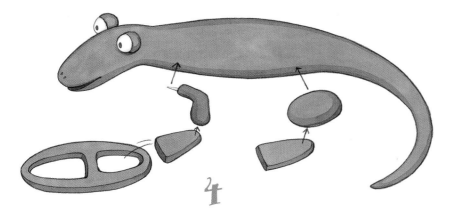

4. Make a sheet and cut out four feet. To make the back legs, join the foot to an oval-shaped ball. For the front legs, join a bent bottle-shaped sausage onto each foot. Stick the four feet onto the body with toothpicks.

5. Mark folds in the back legs. Stick four pieces of plastic tube into each foot to make the toes.

6. To finish, mark the skin texture with a piece of mesh.

Grasshopper

1. Join three pieces together: a triangle for the nose, a flattened ball for the head, and a thick sausage, flat at one end and pointed at the other, for the body. Bend the point upward slightly.

1

2. Smooth the nose joint. Mark lines around the body with a toothpick.

2

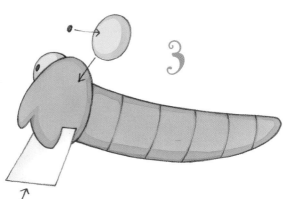

3

3. For the eyes, stick two little balls onto two larger balls and stick them on the head. Make the mouth under the nose with a piece of cardboard.

4. Cut out two paper wings and stick them on the body. Place a piece of a clay sheet on top of the wings to hold them on.

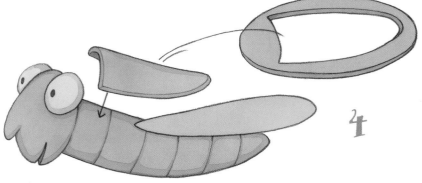

4

5. Paint six pieces of toothpick for the legs. Stick the two front legs straight into the body. Stick the two pairs of back legs into small sausages and then stick the sausage ends into the body.

6. For the antennae, stick two pieces of fishing line onto two little balls.

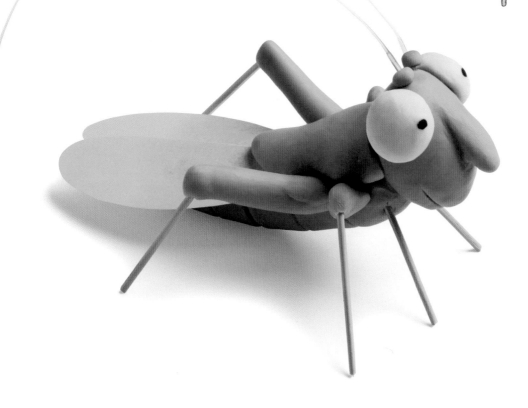

A true athlete

Grasshoppers are known for their jumping ability. Sometimes, they "play tricks" and use their wings to cover great distances.

Modeling Clay
Animals

First edition for the United States and Canada published
in 2010 by Barron's Educational Series, Inc.
© Copyright 2010 by Gemser Publications S.L.
C/Castell, 38; Teià (08329) Barcelona, Spain (World Rights)
Author and illustrator: Bernadette Cuxart

All inquiries should be addressed to:
Barron's Educational Series, Inc.
250 Wireless Boulevard
Hauppauge, NY 11788
www.barronseduc.com

ISBN-13: 978-0-7641-4579-7
ISBN-10: 0-7641-4579-7

Library of Congress Control Number: 2010924487

Date of Manufacture: July 2010
Manufactured by: L. Rex Printing Co. Ltd., TinWan, Aberdeen, Hong Kong

Printed in China
9 8 7 6 5 4 3 2 1